BROADWAY MEN

CONTENTS

Put On A Happy Face

from "Bye Bye Birdie"

Words and Music by
Lee Adams and Charles Strouse

5

MMO 2149

Try To Remember

from "The Fantasticks"

Words and Music by
Tom Jones and Harvey Schmidt

1. Try to re-mem-ber the kind of Sep-tem-ber when life was so and oh, so mel-low.____ Try to re-mem-ber the kind of Sep-tem-ber when grass was green and grain was yel-low.____ Try to re-mem-ber the kind of Sep-tem-ber when you were a ten-der and cal-low fel-low.____ Try to re-mem-ber, and if you re-mem-ber, then fol-low.____

2. Try to re-mem-ber when life was so ten-der that no one wept ex-cept the wil-low.____ Try to re-mem-ber when life was so ten-der that dreams were kept be-side your pil-low.____ Try to re-mem-ber when life was so ten-der that love was an em-ber a-bout to bil-low.____ Try to re-mem-ber, and if you re-mem-ber, then fol-low.____

3. Deep in De-cem-ber, it's nice to re-mem-ber al-though you know the snow will fol-low.____ Deep in De-cem-ber, it's nice to re-mem-ber with-out a hurt, the heart is hol-low.____ Deep in De-cem-ber, it's nice to re-mem-ber the fire of Sep-tem-ber that made us mel-low.____ Deep in De-cem-ber, our hearts should re-mem-ber and fol-low.____

I Believe In You

from "How To Succeed In Business Without Really Trying"

**Words and Music by
Frank Loesser**

8

Lucky To Be Me

On The Town

Words and Music by
**Betty Comden, Adolph Green
and Leonard Bernstein**

MMO 2149

I Won't Send Roses

from "Mack and Mabel"

Words and Music by
Jerry Herman

MMO 2149

The Yankee Doodle Boy

Words and Music by
George M Cohan

Ramapo Music Publishing (BMI)

MMO 2149

Stranger In Paradise

from "Kismet"

Words and Music by
Robert Wright and George Forrest

MMO 2149

And This Is My Beloved
from "Kismet"

Words and Music by
Robert Wright and George Forrest

Note: this contrapuntal piece is originally performed by multiple singers; however, the main melodic line shown here may be sung by one singer.

Marsinah (M)   Caliph (C)   Poet (P)   Wazir (W)

(dialog)   *colla voce*   You'd say his eyes were... Some time bright.

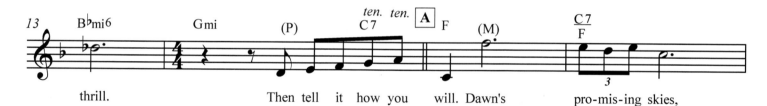

But on-ly some-times... Of-ten dark. Well, that is plain... Plain words can't tell the

thrill.   Then tell it how you will. Dawn's   pro-mis-ing skies,

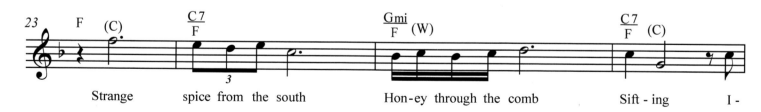

Pe-tals on a pool, drift-ing. Im - a-gine this,— in one pair of eyes, And this is my be-lov-ed.

Strange   spice from the south   Hon-ey through the comb   Sift - ing   I-

ma-gine this_____ on one ea-ger mouth   And this is my be - lov - ed.

Ordinary People

from "Kwamina"

Words and Music by Richard Adler

Other Great Vocals from Music Minus One

**Vol. 1 - Sing the Songs of
George & Ira Gershwin**......................................MMO 2101
Somebody Loves Me • The Man I Love • Bidin' My Time • Someone To Watch Over Me • I've Got A Crush On You • But Not For Me • S'Wonderful • Fascinatin' Rhythm

Vol. 2 - Sing the Songs of Cole Porter............................MMO 2102
Night And Day • You Do Something To Me • Just One Of Those Things • Begin The Beguine • What Is This Thing Called Love • Let's Do It • Love For Sale • I Get A Kick Out Of You

Vol. 3 - Sing the Songs of Irving Berlin.........................MMO 2103
Cheek To Cheek • Steppin' Out With My Baby • Let's Face The Music And Dance • Change Partners • Let Yourself Go • Say It Isn't So • Isn't This A Lovely Day • This Year's Kisses • Be Careful, It's My Heart

Vol. 4 - Sing the Songs of Harold Arlen.........................MMO 2104
I've Got The World On A String • Down With Love • As Long As I Live • Stormy Weather • I've Got A Right To Sing The Blues • The Blues In The Night • Out Of This World • Come Rain Or Come Shine • My Shining Hour • Hooray For Love

Vol. 5 - Sing More Songs by George & Ira Gershwin, Vol. 2 .....MMO 2105
Of Thee I Sing • Embraceable You • Oh, Lady Be Good • How Long Has This Been Going On? • Summertime • Love Walked In • Nice Work If You Can Get It • I Got Rhythm

Vol. 6 - Sing the Songs of Duke Ellington ....MMO 2106
Do Nothin' Until You Hear From Me • I Got It Bad (And That Ain't Good) • I Let A Song Go Out Of My Heart • It Don't Mean A Thing (If It Ain't Got That Swing) • Mood Indigo • Solitude • Sophisticated Lady • Don't Get Around Much Anymore

Vol. 7 - Sing the Songs of Fats Waller ....MMO 2107
I'm Gonna Sit Right Down And Write Myself A Letter • I've Got A Feeling I'm Falling • Squeeze Me • S'posin' • Two Sleepy People • Ain't Misbehavin' (I'm Savin' My Love For You) • Honeysuckle Rose • I Can't Give You Anything But Love • It's A Sin To Tell A Lie

Vol. 8 - Sing the Songs of Cole Porter, Vol. 2 ....MMO 2108
You're The Top • Easy To Love • Friendship • Anything Goes • Blow, Gabriel, Blow • You're The Top (Jazz Version) • I Get A Kick Out Of You • Anything Goes (Jazz Version)

Vol. 9 - Sing the Songs of Jimmy McHugh ....MMO 2109
It's A Most Unusual Day • You're a Sweetheart • Don't Blame Me • I Feel A Song Coming On • I'm in the Mood for Love • I Can't Give You Anything But Love • I Can't Believe That You're in Love with Me • On the Sunny Side of the Street • I Must Have That Man

Vol. 10 - Sing the Songs of Jerome Kern ....MMO 2110
A Fine Romance • Smoke Gets In Your Eyes • The Last Time I Saw Paris • The Way You Look Tonight • Yesterdays • The Folks Who Live On The Hill • Make Believe • I'm Old Fashioned • All The Things You Are • They Didn't Believe Me

Vol. 11 - Sing the Songs of Johnny Mercer ....MMO 2111
Come Rain or Come Shine • Charade • The Days of Wine and Roses • Dream • I'm Old Fashioned • I Wanna Be Around • Jeepers Creepers • Moon River • One For My Baby

Vol. 12 - Sing the Songs of Johnny Mercer, Vol. 2 ....MMO 2112
The Autumn Leaves • Fools Rush In • I Remember You • My Shining Hour • Skylark • Tangerine • Too Marvelous For Words • Mr. Meadowlark

Vol. 13 - Sing the Songs of Rodgers & Hart ....MMO 2113
I Didn't Know What Time It Was • My Funny Valentine • Nobody's Heart Belongs To Me • A Ship Without A Sail • Dancing On The Ceiling • It Never Entered My Mind • There's A Small Hotel • Where Or When

Vol. 14 - Sing the Songs of Harry Warren........................MMO 2114
You'll Never Know • The More I See You • I Wish I Knew • This Is Always • I Had The Craziest Dream • I Only Have Eyes For You • Jeepers Creepers • That's Amore • Serenade In Blue

Music Minus One
50 Executive Boulevard • Elmsford, New York 10523-1325
914-592-1188 • e-mail: info@musicminusone.com
www.musicminusone.com

MMO 2149

ISBN 978-1-941566-49-7